SKETCHBOOK
PARIS

STORIES, JOURNAL/COLORING BOOK
(A book you can make your own)

DEAMER DUNN

DEAMER DUNN artbz.bz

PARIS is unique in its neighborhood distinction that follows the twenty administrative districts created in 1859. There are a few neighborhood identities such as *Vavin, Pigalle* and *Faubourg* that cross arrondissement lines, but for the most part, residents and businesses identify with the arrondissement of their location. This Sketchbook is arranged by most of these districts: one through twelve, plus fourteen and eighteen. Each section has a story which relates to one or more of the sketches inspired within each arrondissement. No need for me to suggest Paris's unique world status. You all know it before you ever visit. Is Paris still the world's most romantic city? I still notice more couples openly kissing and touching as I walk its streets. Or, do we just notice such things because of this city's reputation? Take this book along for your next visit and/or let it take you from wherever you are.

Copyright © 2025 Deamer Dunn

All rights reserved. No part of this publication may be reproduced in any form or by any means without written permission from the publishers Deamer Dunn and Pajaro Street Inc.

Available to resellers through:

KDP
ISBN-13: 979884742280

INGRAM SPARK
ISBN-13:

Editor: Dani Cyrer

All Art by Deamer

First Addition
Pajaro Street Inc

SKETCHBOOK – PARIS

Book Notes & Disclosures

Most of my sketch victims were unaware that my camera, eye and pencil clad fingers had focused upon them. For the most part, the tales I write for this series of sketchbooks are on individuals I know nothing of, beyond what I observed from drawing them. Consider these as bonus material for inspiring you to make this book your own.

The drawings of this Sketchbook are organized by their corresponding Paris arrondissement. Fourteen of these neighborhoods are represented. I had extra fun with my Paris books by relating the fictional short stories here with the plot of my novel, 'Omar T in Paris.' I also published an additional Paris book in this series, 'SKETCHBOOK MUSEE D'ORSAY.' All these drawings are within and near the museum's surroundings.

OMAR T IN PARIS: Chef Omar heads to the city of love to help with the food service for the film, 'Paris Fourteen.' This collection of short films is shot in each of the first 12 Paris arrondissements as well as the 14th & 18th. Romance blossoms on and off screen. ABOUT THE SERIES: Omar and his family travel to a different location for each of these culinary adventures. The travel fiction aspect is enhanced with descriptions of actual sites, restaurants, bookstores, galleries and shops—including sketches, favorite lists and recipes. Diversity in race, religion, culture, language and sexual orientation not only exists within Omar's family, it is celebrated in these tales. Each Omar T book is independent, you do not need to read them in the order of their publication, though, as the collection grows, there are more references between the novels.

Artist/Author Deamer Dunn
Author Web Site: http://artbz.bz
Amazon Author Page: https://www.amazon.com/author/deamerdunn
(Please pass on your impressions; write a review on Amazon and/or other sites)
You can also support your local bookstore via: https://bookshop.org/shop/deamerdunn

YouTube Author/Artist Page (music videos of art & book sketches):
https://www.youtube.com/@deamerdunn
https://www.instagram.com/deamerauthor/
Friend me on Facebook: Deamer Dunn Author
I would love to hear from you: deamer@artbz.bz

DEAMER DUNN artbz.bz

As a Journal/Coloring Book:
A BOOK YOU CAN MAKE YOUR OWN

In case you haven't heard, coloring books for all ages are becoming quite a passion. Perhaps, for many, a little coloring can still feed a passion for getting into a book, as well as allowing the satisfaction of finishing something. A few of these sketches are accompanied with a fictional story influenced by the scene. Deamer Sketchbooks are meant to inspire you. Each sketch is partnered with a blank page—you can add notes, comments, poems, words of a song, or your own artistic doodles—innovation inspired by creative human activity. The idea is that this is a book that you can make your own. It is a travel companion, whether you take it along, or it takes you…

Cheers! *Salud! A Votre Sante! Saluti!*

Contents, by Arrondissement

Page	Arrondissement
PAGE 6	1st
34	2nd
48	3rd
68	4th
92	5th
106	6th
128	7th
142	8th
152	9th
160	10th
172	11th
186	12th
200	14th
220	18th

236 APPENDIX OF IMAGES
238 DEAMER BOOKS
240 ABOUT THE AUTHOR

1ˢᵗ **Arrondissement**

Ah, the 1ˢᵗ arrondissement of Paris. The river *Seine, Pont Neuf, Sainte-Chapelle Cathedral, Île de la Cité,* and the *Musée du Louvre,* the former royal palace filled with priceless art—its glass pyramid addition, the adjoining gardens of the *Jardin des Tuileries, Place Vendome,* its 'Ritzy' shops and its signature hotel. Speaking of shopping, there is *Les Halles* for everyone, and the Saturday market at *Saint-Honoré* for us locals. Many a tourist thinks of something within the first when they first think of Paris. You even get views of two of Paris's most iconic structures, the *Eiffel Tower* and *Le Cathedral of Notre Dame.* What this center of Paris means to me is work. I don't say this to be derogatory, I'm very thankful for the type of labor that this arrondissement offers to me. I work security at the *Ritz Hotel,* the *Louvre* and at the hub of all of the transit of Paris, *Châtelet.* I'm the son of a baker who was worked those brutal baker hours all of his life. He could have never imagined his son hanging out in such high-brow places, as well as mingling with the super-rich. Dad was good at what he did and he had an unparalleled work ethic, but, such demanding labors, combined with a cigarette at every break, brought his life to an early end. I was determined not to fall into his profession, I longed for something less physical and more connected to the world. I've worked just about every type of hospitality job, which not only taught me the skills of service, I was also exposed to so many interesting people. I found myself questioning those that I had met, learning their stories. Before I had even noticed a change in the shy behavior of my youth, I was engaging with all kinds of people on a daily basis. The move to security came gradually. The change to a position of more authority didn't stop me from my new favorite profession, storytelling. For all of these years, I've been asking questions and once in a while someone has told me something worthy of repeating. Somewhere along the line, I became a pretty good storyteller myself. I really enjoy taking in the reactions, as I tell others the good stories that I've been told. Whether I'm directing people through the maze of *Châtelet,* the endless inventory of the *Louvre,* or in the lobby of the Ritz, I've found how appreciative are my fellow humans of a good tale—whether they are refugees to my country or someone whose clothing for the day cost more than I make in a year. I think of all of those decades that my father had spent building, caressing and taming a ferocious fire so that people could have their daily bread. You could almost count the number of words that were used in our conversations as he would tend to his burnt and callused hands. Just yesterday, I had a woman from Algeria, explain to me a custom of her country, while that afternoon a man at the Ritz, patiently shared the meaning of the French expression *eau de vie,* the water of life. He explained, "Yes, you might find it printed on a bottle of water, or even have a spirit such as brandy referred to as an *eau de vie*. But its bigger meaning, he explained, is a way of living—feeding your mind, body and spirit in a way that makes life worth living." Somehow, I don't think that the words *eau de vie* ever trickled off my father's gravel tongue— let alone he comprehending a more esoteric meaning. I think that he only understood a Frenchman's need of bread with every meal, not the concept of feeding a grander spirit…

JARDIN DES TUILERIES

5/2022

SKETCHBOOK – PARIS

SKETCHBOOK – PARIS

SKETCHBOOK – PARIS

19

SKETCHBOOK – PARIS

SKETCHBOOK – PARIS

SKETCHBOOK – PARIS

SKETCHBOOK – PARIS

SKETCHBOOK – PARIS

2nd Arrondissement

There are still those who believe that an actress is just a glorified whore. Given my history, this just makes me laugh. I do get off on acting, playing a role and listening to the applause. Afterall, I am a third-generation resident of the second arrondissement. The second has always been a draw for its entertainment. Like all of Paris, we have our share of brasseries and cafes. What has drawn Parisians and tourists to our sector for centuries is our particular accent on entertainment. We were home to the first theater of Paris, Hôtel de Bourgogne, which was built on a portion of the ruins of the residences of the Dukes of Burgundy, in the mid-sixteen hundreds. Present day, the second is still rich in theaters. These are spread throughout the arrondissement Look around as you walk through the second. You won't have to go far before you see a marker announcing that inside is the workings of drama. There is a particular concentration in the western half. The east, Rue Sentier and Rue St. Denis is known more for its open-air entertainment that is found in its boisterous crowds, which flow in and out, around all of its bars. And, well, there is the history of Rue St. Denis, of which my grandmother was a participant. Before the Internet and all of the connecting of social media, the so-called 'oldest profession' was a known reality of Rue St. Denis. From what I understand, the sex worker was a part of the scene on Saint Denis for centuries. This was the life of my grandmother, who apparently had quite the career, before and after my mother was born. I have vague memories of her prior to her passing. I remember that she still liked to dress up and that she would laugh all of the time. She would talk and then talk some more, always telling me stories. I wasn't old enough to understand or retain the things that she would share, though, I do remember her good humor and especially her laugh. We still live in the same apartment on Rue St. Denis, above the store that my grandmother started and turned over to my mother. Ok, it is a sex-shop, but we also sell lingerie, which seems to make it feel a little more legit. Not that you must be respectful to be on rue Saint Denis. Along with all of the trendy cafes and bars, we have several sex-shops and even a few 'peep shows.' True to its history, this section of the second is still always active and vibrant. Apparently, the shop was my grandmother's idea of allowing my mother to make a different living. Unlike my grandmother, my mother doesn't like to talk about the past. She is more interested in being an efficient shop owner.

I don't know if growing up in this environment has led me to the theater, but it just seems natural that it contributed. In the neighborhood, I met a lot of thespians, who encouraged me to pursue roles. I've participated in productions in a great many of the theaters of the Second. I'm very excited about a role that I have just landed at the *Théâtre des Bouffes-Parisiens* on Rue Monsigny. I've always wanted to work in this historic and elaborate theater. I'm also interested in the other members of the production. There seems to be something about my life that makes me particularly built for doing a comedy, *une comédie*.

Coming from a line of single mothers, men have always been a mystery to me. Nothing against my grandmother or mother, but I have to admit that I have this dream of a different life. Could it be due to all of the fantasy that I live in as an actress? I keep imagining that I live in this cottage in the country, with a couple of kids running around me and a caring spouse. Though, if I'm being honest with you, I still have a problem with deciding on the gender of my future partner. As much as I'm drawn to the mystery of men, I find the idea of living with one rather overwhelming…

SKETCHBOOK – PARIS

SKETCHBOOK – PARIS

SKETCHBOOK – PARIS

SKETCHBOOK – PARIS

SKETCHBOOK – PARIS

SKETCHBOOK – PARIS

3rd Arrondissement

There was something about the third arrondissement that attracted me. Perhaps, it was because it used to be a Jewish quarter and home to other immigrant populations. There are still remnants of a Chinatown and it is very easy to find cuisine from all over the world. It didn't really resonate with me, until I heard an American friend explain the expression, "the underdog." Coming from another land this phrase summed up a feeling that had been growing inside of me, as I adapted to my adopted home. Not only did I feel like an underdog, but I also felt that I had ended up in a quarter that felt like it was also fighting for recognition and respect. Associating Jewish history with being an underdog is rather an understatement. Though, like all people who have known repression, I think that there is a positive analogy with the spirit of the underdog. Ever since that American friend explained this terminology, I have seen the third arrondissement in a different illumination. This light is synonymous with the life that I and my little family have been building.

The third has its own museums: the *Picasso*, the *Carnavalet*, *L'histoire de Judaisme*, and *Le Cognacq-Jay*, though they have to fight for recognition in this city of museums. We have some beautiful cathedrals. Two of them are a stone's throw from each other. We have some very nice parks. I am particularly fond of the *Jardins du Anne Frank*. If you knew my family history you would understand why I identify with Anne's legend. We may not have the famous cafés that the other parts of Paris, but we have our share of places which offer ambiance, and likely, more variety of food choices. Hey, how about that, did you notice how I'm using the word 'we,' when I talk of this neighborhood? Wow, that is a special realization for this person who has traveled so far, to finally feel such a connection.

My husband and I started out by selling things on the street in the more tourist friendly parts of Paris. It didn't take long for us to return to the love that we had found in our home country, cooking and selling food. It was a slow, but gradual process. We built relationships and grew to the point of opening a mini restaurant. It is located in the heart of the third, *Marche des Enfants Rouge*. This covered, open-air market, dates back to the early sixteen hundreds. When I discovered this unique collection of businesses, positioned within a city, which has a long history of supporting the street markets, I felt something in my heart jump. It didn't take long for me to know this is where we wanted to end up. But it wasn't easy, and it is still a battle. There were already a variety of ethnic businesses that were operating in the Marche, so we felt a degree of comfort being a part of that family. But running a business anywhere has challenges, especially when you are adapting to a very different culture. The best news, is that for the most part, all of the businesses within the *Marche des Enfants Rouge,* know that individual successes help with everyone's overall success. This attitude has really helped us to improve and grow our business. Oh sure, there is a degree of competition amongst us. I have to also admit to being a little jealous of the busy businesses, especially among us restaurants. But, overall, it has been a real blessing for our family to survive and grow into this family of businesses. There are still slow days, customer complaints and even an occasional

SKETCHBOOK – PARIS

divisive comment from a racist. We've been toughened by all of this. We remain thankful that this country, this city and this neighborhood of the underdog, gave us a new opportunity in life. Our operations seem rather simple compared to our "big brother" businesses, such as the grocers, the fromager and such. They have to deal with so many venders and other complications. We just try and make a few really good dishes and serve them all with a smile. We are also blessed with much less overhead than all of those independent cafes and restaurants. They have so many things to worry about. For quite some time we struggled with how the Marche´, rain or shine, is always closed on Mondays. The concept of a day off is rather foreign to us immigrants. Now, I can't imagine living without a day to rest, recover and reflect. Does this make me more French?

There are difficult times with the culture, our business, marriage, and children, but I have found some tools for getting past the ugly and concentrating on the beautiful. I already mentioned visiting a park and there is nothing quite like sitting in a Parisian café, nursing a beverage and watching Paris live. I have another little secret that I will share with you. I guess that you could say that I really felt that I had found my new home when I crossed through all the traffic to *Place de la République*. Its everyday existence, as an important metro stop and traffic circle, is an analogy to us Parisians, as we go about our daily lives. What moves me and keeps me coming back, is its memorial to sacrifice. Its representation of the three things that we could not find in our country back home: Liberty, Equality and Fraternity. It has become a habit of mine, when I am feeling down or I have to make a difficult decision, to again cross through the noise and danger of traffic and immerse myself within this monument's dedication to *Liberté, égalité et fraternité*. Commitments which are a foundation for goodness, and the ideals, which we risked everything for…

SKETCHBOOK – PARIS

SKETCHBOOK – PARIS

SKETCHBOOK – PARIS

SKETCHBOOK – PARIS

SKETCHBOOK – PARIS

SKETCHBOOK – PARIS

4th Arrondissement

I knew that my return to Paris would be different. I'm not sure exactly what I expected. I had some misgivings. I started by visiting the *Cathedral of Notre Dame*. The world came ever so close to losing this icon of Paris. The infrastructure that was in place to restore it from its 2019 fire was very impressive—the enormous crane, all the scaffolding, as well as the temporary support buildings that resemble a small town. It was all blocked off of course. Maneuvering the temporary obstacles and street sellers added some confusion to my now all too often disoriented mind. I thought of how disappointed my wife would have been, since she couldn't go inside and light a candle for her grandmother. It was a simple ritual that helped her keep an attachment to one of her special relations. The steps for renewal were wonderfully described on a section of the wall barrier. I also enjoyed the addition of cartoon like murals, which lightened the sense of loss, as well as thanking those around the world, who had contributed to the Cathedral renewal. I chuckled, thinking that this trip was in a way an effort of renewal for me—I was still working out my plan. Next on my agenda was to see if I could find the unique space that had housed us on our last visit to Paris. We had befriended an American author who split his time 50/50 between California and Paris. He had an apartment rental, just a block from the *Cathedral Notre Dame*. When we heard he was having a celebration for the publishing of his latest book, 'How to Creatively Loiter in Paris," we took up his offer and rented this place. I knew it would be difficult to find, since what I remembered was only the beautiful courtyard that you entered via a gate. I did a painting of my wife and me walking on its interior cobblestones, surrounded by the inner wall, which was drenched in deep green ivy. I did pass a potential candidate, which had the same teal blue color, on its entry that was in my painting. Nowhere else on the street seemed a possibility, so I returned to the blue gate. A group of five folks happened to be gathered in front and they were speaking English. I asked if they might be staying inside the gate. The answer was no, so they could not help me with my attempted identification. I showed them the image of my painting of the courtyard. I went on to explain my wife's passing and that I was on a journey of trying to find the spots that had inspired me to record them with paint and canvas. They wished me luck, as I headed toward the next location, which was the restaurant of La Reserve de Quasimodo, 4 rue de la Colombe. It had been the site of our friend Jeff's book celebration. I had its address, but a google search stated it as permanently closed. I surmised that it was another of many business casualties that were due to the pandemic of 2020. A new restaurant, *Les Deux Colombes*, had taken its place. It had changed the interior enough, so I was having difficulty relating my painting image to the new interior. Jeff's wife's niece, Lila, who was a professional dancer, gave us a little show during the celebration. I later created a painting of her dancing among us inside the restaurant. A kind server, who noticed my look of befuddlement, came outside and asked if she could help me. I mixed English and French well enough to explain, which to my surprise, inspired her eyes to get glossy. She told me a little about the new restaurant and ended up giving me a hug. Clearly, a woman, like my wife, who beautifully, do not attempt to hide their emotions. Next up, was to walk the bridge between *Ile de le Cite* and *Ile de Saint*

SKETCHBOOK – PARIS

Louis and return to *Café Le Flore*. There were no worries of this historic café disappearing or ending its timeless tradition of serving Berthillon ice cream. On this warm spring day, my wife would have ordered a sorbet, so I asked for a combo of this refreshing dessert.

I crossed over the Seine again, tipping the musician, who was working for some tips. He had set-up residence in the place that I had planned to take a selfie. It was in this spot, that my wife and I had taken a picture of us, with the river Seine and Paris in the background. A copy of us in this scene, still hangs in our bedroom. Back then, we had taken five different shots with our camera, hoping to obtain at least one great picture. We did not have the luxury of checking out the quality instantly, like we do now with digital images. My selfie idea was exchanged for the good cheer of the guitarist's tones and calming voice. My next stop was *Rue Barres*, which is a most unusual hidden pathway, that you could easily walk right by, without ever knowing its existence. The entry is somewhat camouflaged among all of the restaurant outdoor seating and umbrellas of Chez Julien. Its unique, slow rising cobblestones, start wide, and then narrow, as you get near the ancient church and quaint aged apartments at its end. What made it such a visual treat was the old stone that contrasted with the bold colors of the restaurants and the greenery. Except for the most dominant green, the ivy that had reached all the way up to the fourth floor of the apartments was gone. As I held up the image of my painting, filled with green, comparing it to the faded white in front of me, I felt a strong pain of loss. I felt an ugly symmetry between myself and all that was left of what had once been magnificent ivy, and now was only the dried out brown stocks of the vine. At first, I thought that maybe, its spring green just hadn't arrived yet, but it became clear from the breaks that were visible, that it had died. A few of the men working at the outdoor restaurant, *L'Ébouillanté*, which I was standing in the middle of, checked out my painting image and nodded their heads in approval.

The emotion so overcame me that I finally sat at one of their small bistro tables. It was another young woman server who showed me some empathy, which helped me to come back into what was still a beautiful present. She asked to see the painting and gave me some lovely compliments. All of the life that was in her big hair and her youthful girlishness, helped to restore my attitude and resolve.

From *Rue Barres*, I wandered through some parts of the fourth that I didn't really remember well, looking for another centerpiece of this arrondissement, the *Hotel de Ville*. I was reminded of the expression the 'Gay Marias' as I came across a section of rainbow painted sidewalks and umbrellas, along with some creative expression that was found in many shop names, as well as décor that related to the LBGQT community. My spirit continued to mend, with what was clearly a much more open and expressive show, of a more tolerant world. This was something that both my wife and I had always hoped for. As I went around a few corners I discovered a couple of other businesses that made me smile. *La Cerise Sur La Pizza* was not only fun, in that it made the most of an awkward corner construction. It spoke to my heart with their big sign that stated, "Just Believe in Art." I also cracked up upon seeing the business named *Bien Fait*. This was not only because I love this expression that translates to 'well done.' I chuckled at the thought of how it would be a good image for just about any type of business. Its subtitle was, "*Editor de Decors Singul*," which I roughly translated to be 'Single scenery editor.' I had to think a minute before concluding, "Ah, a decorator." This seemed correct as I took in the patterned painting of its front, and also the rolls of material that were displayed.

I had to pull out my phone to get myself headed back in the correct direction. I found the *Hotel de Ville*, home to the mayor of Paris, as well as its grand plaza. I got a kick out of the diverse crowd that was hanging around its fountains. They all seemed to especially appreciate the serenity of the flowing waters. In contrast to this simple joy, attached to the iron fencing, were images and descriptions of some of the plight that was being caused by Russia's invasion of Ukraine. Again, I was moved to tears, and this time thinking of others who were suffering from our human limitations. Last on my list was a place that had been most special to my wife. Her beautiful heart and high intellect, had shared her interior with an equally intense sense of anxiety. Her nervousness was sometimes so overwhelming that she had to find the nearest tree. She would put her hands on its aged structure and calm herself down. She had been a top of class student in virtually all disciplines, including French. But her anxiety had always limited her ability to adventure on her own and make use of her language skills. On our last trip to Paris, something had clicked in her confidence. Each morning, she started to take a walk on her own. Once she had discovered the *Place to Vosges* and its regal feeling and all of the majestic trees, it became her morning destination. She would return with fresh goodies for me and tales of joy—stories of her immersing with the nature of *Place de Vosges*. Before moving on to making some new discoveries, I chose as many trees, as the years that she had been gone, placing my hands on them and giving them thanks for their gift to us all, especially how they had inspired and calmed the love of my life.

When I had approached *Rue Barres* earlier, I had noticed some interesting looking businesses to the east that I hadn't remembered ever exploring. It turned out that the name of the street was *Rue de Hotel de Ville*. This section of the road has businesses on one side, and a strip of park on the other. This thin green rectangle is home to a plethora of mature trees, adding to its sense of comfort. I felt an immediate renewal, when I realized that the three places that were sporting outdoor tables were a bookstore, a wine bar and a coffee house—three of my favorite things living side-by-side. I thought first a coffee and then a peek in the bookstore, followed by a glass of wine. *Caféotheque* (see book cover) was a rather unusual Paris café. Each of its multiple rooms are different in look and feel. Its heart is centered around the coffee bean roaster and the selection of more than twenty different coffees for sale. I took my cappuccino outside and settled into one of the funky bistro tables that was facing the Seine. There were no views of the river from this neighboring plot, but a smile came to my face as I could see Notre Dame's twin towers perfectly between the branches and green leaves in front of me. I had started my day in front of the iconic Cathedral that had come ever so close to being pronounced dead itself. Now, like me, we were starting anew, and getting refreshed. I maneuvered my table until it settled relatively stable on its cobblestone pavement. I took out my sketchbook and opened my phone to the photos that I had taken on my day of rediscovering the 4th arrondissement. Much had changed, and some things had disappeared. Now, I was sitting somewhere new and exciting. I blew a kiss to the cosmos, pulled out a pencil and started working on some new memories…

SKETCHBOOK – PARIS

SKETCHBOOK – PARIS

SKETCHBOOK – PARIS

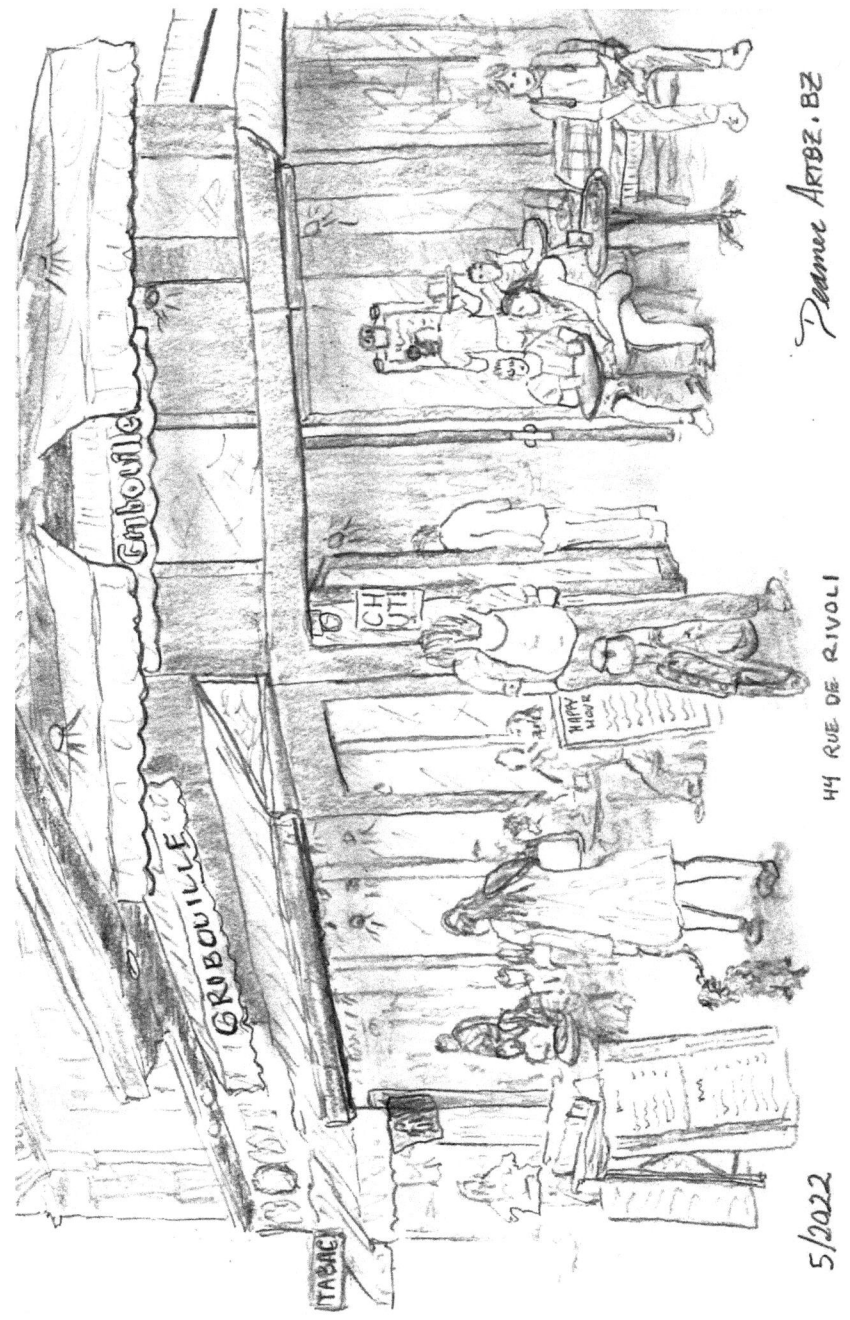

SKETCHBOOK – PARIS

SKETCHBOOK – PARIS

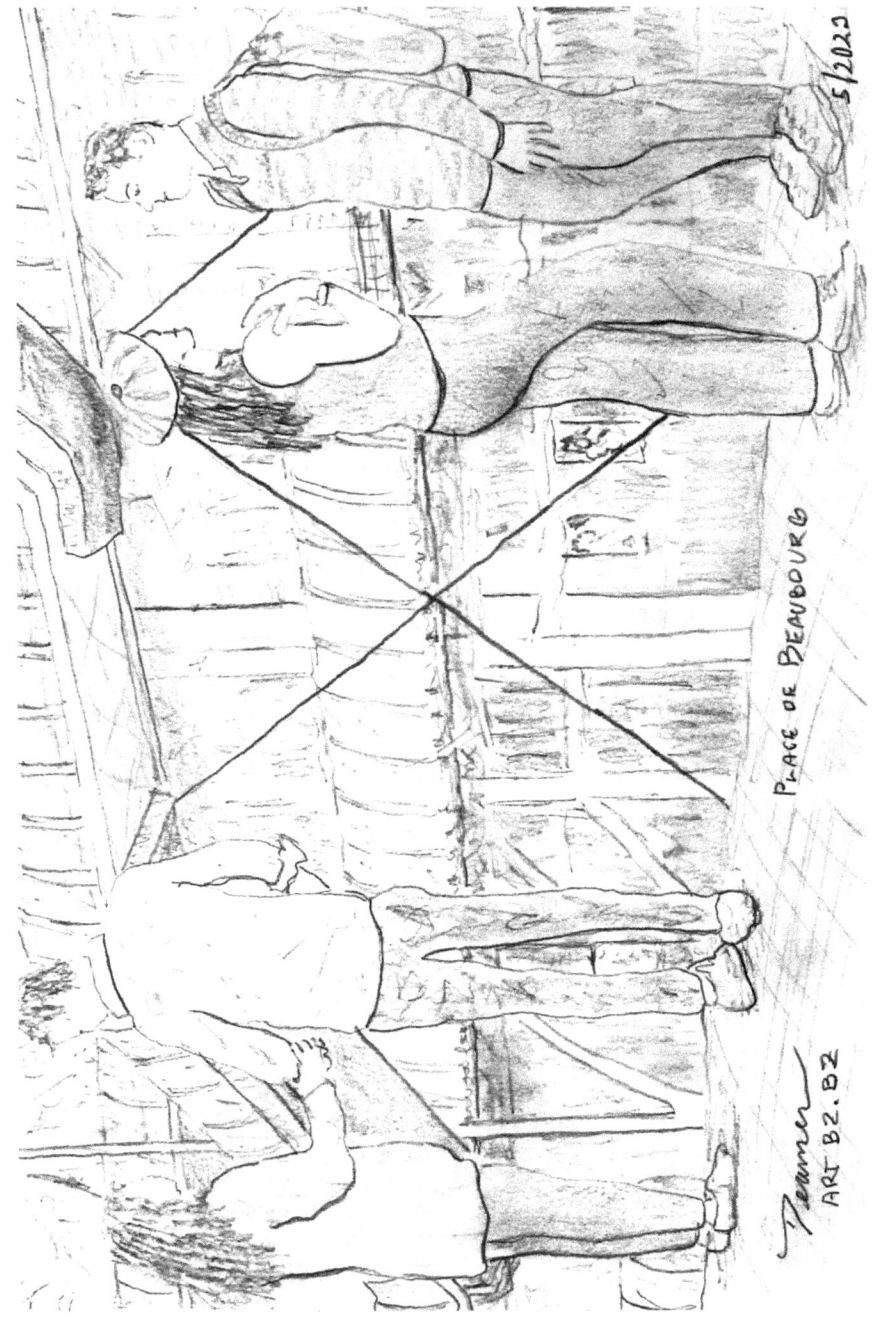

SKETCHBOOK – PARIS

5th Arrondissement

Have you ever thought about how thin the threads of our life can be? I was one of those kids that was born into a predetermined life. I am not like a young woman in a rural village somewhere that is still struggling to join the twenty-first century. No, I was born and raised right in the middle of one of the world's most famous cities. Like many a kid that is born into a family run business, the path of the lives of myself and my two siblings was always known to be through the family business. After all, we not only sell fruits and vegetables on the famed Paris market street, *Rue Mouffetard*, but we also have, for generations, lived above the store. As soon as we were old enough, we helped with its operation. Even in our cribs that were in the store, we were a part of it. Especially my sister; who was pretty and social from the beginning. Once it was established that I was the 'smart one,' the family expectations became clearer and clearer, as I made my way up the educational chain. My brother was the athlete, and my sister was either the beauty, the sexy one or the whore—depending on who you talked to. I wonder how much each of us grew into the role of the perceived expectations…

I'm sure that my brother struggled somewhat with the transition from being a good footballer to being dad's right-hand man, but he was never one to discuss anything so deep. He seemed to being content with ordering around his younger siblings and any of our staff, especially when dad or mom were not on site. My sister seemed happy to flirt with all of the daily visitors, which selling produce brings. She seems to thrive in an environment that brings in a constant stream of eligible men. I guess that I'm such a nerd that I didn't even notice the transition from when dad and mom seemed concerned with men that were flirting with my sister. It suddenly dawned on me one day that my parents no longer seemed to protect her virtue. They just joined in with all the vamp talk and laughter. Anyway, I was the one to continue my education beyond Lycée. Even though, I would end up being, the first in the family line to gain a higher education, it was not considered a big deal. I took over the shop's bookkeeping in high school. It was all logical and easy for me. My parents' expectations of what I would gain from being more educated was always blurry in its concept, but its application was always known to be toward helping the business grow and prosper.

There were other kids in the neighborhood who went on to study at the Sorbonne or the University of Paris. After all, we didn't even have to leave the 5th arrondissement to attend these elevated educational institutes. Even though my university was just down the hill, I also began to get some education in ways of living other than what I knew growing up on Rue Mouffetard. It was more than learning about other cultures, we've had quite an ethnic mix on Mouffetard most of my life. It was more about an exposure to different types of identity and styles of living. My new best friend happened to be Muslim. I learned a lot by seeing things through her eyes. We had a wonderful routine at the end of each day of study. We would walk and talk our way up the hill, with her veering off to the great mosque, just before I entered my world of Rue Mouffetard. We both feared about how our traditional families would react when they understood our ideas of a different life.

My future began to reshape rather innocently. Like a dutiful produce business child, I began to take courses in the sciences. I wanted to understand more of what was behind the fruits and vegetables that my family had been selling for generations. My interest in micro biotics and the upcoming needs of feeding the world, also seemed like just another extension of preparing the family business for our future. Well, that is how it started. Turns out that the 'smart one' actually has a mind for science. Who would have thought? The deeper I delved into the world of micro biotics, the more that I realized that I had found a home away from the world of transactions. This fascination, no I will now call it love, may have faded away just like a ripened fruit that doesn't get eaten, if not for Professor Miloy. It was she that took me by the hand and literally walked me back up the hill that I had walked down every day on my way to the Sorbonne. I had passed by IPGG, the *Institut Pierre-Gilles de Gennes*, many times. It is just a block away from our business and home. But it meant nothing to me. You must understand, I have never really left Paris, unless you count some of the farms that I have been to that are just outside the city. In fact, beyond the fifth and maybe the 6th arrondissement, I really do not know well any other parts of Paris. For my family, so much of everything took place in the fifth. You must understand the nature of *Rue Mouffetard*. Thanks to our ongoing street market, it is the rest of Paris that is drawn to us. I do admit that during my junior year, when so many other students began talking about their big plans after university, I began, for the first time, to imagine life beyond the Mouffetard market. There were multiple days that I had gone and had a coffee in the café at the bookstore Shakespeare and Co. I began to feel more connected to the rest of the world, mingling with the tourists, which come from all over the world to enjoy this iconic bookstore. Following my years of studying it, I thought my English pretty good until I tried to speak it—I would get too nervous. I started to buy books in English from this iconic bookstore, to secretly improve my understanding of this language of the world. This ended up being a bonus in my science studies, for English is prevalent, in the language of research and innovation.

After my visit to IPGG, a whole world of possibility had been opened to what I now knew to be a brain of limited exposure. The Institute outlined how I could gain a masters through them and go right into working within their micro world of discovery and innovation. How ironic that I would not need to leave the 5th arrondissement to find the rest of the world. Now, I just have to explain all of this to my mother and father...

SKETCHBOOK – PARIS

6th **Arrondissement**

Paris is a very old city. Tradition has a way of shaping and clouding. My life as a poet, a writer and finally a bookstore creator, has been shaped by this city's history each step of the way. I came to Paris from the countryside to get a higher education. For those who have not grown up in a rural environment, you probably can't imagine the sensory overload of suddenly finding yourself in a city, especially one so connected to the creative human spirit. As I struggled to find myself in this new environment, I stumbled into the genre of poetry. I will never know how much my attraction was to its esoteric quality, and how much was due to the group of students that were drawn to the medium. It was the whole culture that seduced this *naïve* person. The combination of experimentation and breaking of the norm was intoxicating. There was Monique, then Pierre, and well, Julie, Paul and I were a threesome for quite a while. Love, sex and the creative, fed all of these relationships. Gender was very fluid in our world. Poetry was the muse that held us together and pulled us apart.

All of Paris is of course associated with great historical creative creators. When it comes to the art of writing, the sixth arrondissement is, and has been, a focal point. Once graduated, I set about the task of expanding from the luxury of being a student of the arts, to trying to figure out how to make a living. All of us students felt that we could maintain the culture of creativity, while we also participated more in society. But of course, it was different out in the real world. A bunch of us still lived together to keep the cost of rent under control. This did take some pressure off how much we had to earn, but it seemed the increasing responsibility that we all were facing brought on new pressures that damaged our carefree student youth. Some of the wicked j-words seeped into our lives, jealousy and judgement. The illusion that I could make it as just a poet died rather quickly. I switched to prose. I worked in cafes to make money, and then sat much of the rest of the day trying to write. This lifestyle had the benefit of keeping me away from all of the drama at our apartment. For a long time, I felt empowered. I could nurse a *café au lait* for hours, as I pecked away on my laptop. I felt a camaraderie with all of the great writers who had sat in the same cafes when they were also young and living day-to-day. The sixth was important to so many legends, Henry Miller, Hemingway, Faulkner, Fitzgerald, Joyce and Beckett. I tried my best to channel their words into my work. I would often veer from my path to walk down *Rue de Odeon*, to stop below *number 12* and the plaque honoring Sylvia Beach—the original location of the now iconic Shakespeare and Co. Not only was this legendary bookstore the first publisher of many writers, most notably, James Joyce's Ulysses, it has lived long beyond Sylvia. I confess to also sitting outside *27 Rue des Fleures*, former home to Gertrude Stein, the benefactor of so many artists and writers that became known worldwide. The building today is rather undistinguishable, but it was inside its gate that history was being lived and made. Surely, what hung on those walls would now be worth more than a billion euros, And, some of the stories that were born in that apartment, will live forever. It was also not lost on me that both Sylvia and Gertrude, lived

SKETCHBOOK – PARIS

alternative lifestyles, back when gender identity was just trying to make itself to a connecting closet, let alone being out in the open—like it has been for me.

I began to spend a great deal of time within the sixth's bookstores. As much as a bookstore can be found in just about every neighborhood of Paris, I can't imagine that there is a section anywhere in the world, as rich in these peddlers of books as is the sixth. It was not an easy realization to make, but I finally concluded that my writing ability wasn't good enough or productive enough to believe that I would ever be able to join in the history of writing legends. A new dream formed. I wanted to own a bookstore. I spent less time writing, more time working and for the first time in my life, I started saving. At first, I thought I would try to have a place that would particularly support poets. But we already had that with *Poesie/Librairie Galerie Racine* on Rue Racine and the Société *Des Poètes Français* on Rue Monsieur le Prince. We also have the historic shops such as *Librairie Guenegaud* and *Alain Brieux*, as well as a plethora of small, cute bookshops: *Le Coupe Papier, Amelie Sourget, L'inconnu, Monte Cristo, Benoit Forgeot* and *Librairie des Alpes*. There are some more modern versions, such as *Les Immortels* and *Vigot Maloine*, and the specialized ones like *Des Femmes* and the children's fantasy of *Canal BD*. We even have the dedicated *editeur*/publisher with its fun painted windows that resemble stacks of books. There is also *Assouline*, which is very unique. The books and the shop are as elegant as anything in Vogue or Architectural Digest. These high-end collectable Art Book publications are works of art in themselves. I found a space and an American partner. We are going to combine the café culture of our famous *Germain-des-Pres* section of the 6th, with books, our arrondissements historic heart. It is going to take some time, but I hope to have our bookstore café up and running by the next time that you will visit Paris and the Sixth Arrondissement…

SKETCHBOOK – PARIS

SKETCHBOOK – PARIS

SKETCHBOOK – PARIS

SKETCHBOOK – PARIS

7th Arrondissement

I've been trying to figure out how I could sleep on the fifth floor of the *Musée D'Orsay*. Ever since I decided to pursue my love of studying art history, I planned to spend a year abroad in Paris. When I learned that *AUP, American University in Paris* was in the same arrondissement as the D'Orsay, it was a done deal. You see, my particular interest is the second half of the twentieth century and the artists that changed art forever. Manet, Pissarro, Monet, Degas, Renoir, Cezanne, Sisley, Whistler and of course, those who had joined in the revolution a little later, Gauguin, Serut, Signac and Van Gogh. Even with all of my studying, it is still impossible to imagine that all of these giants of art knew each other, painted together, and had long friendships. Italy dominated art during the renaissance. Velasquez dominated art in Spain as it dominated the world. By the mid-nineteenth century, Paris was the undisputed center of the art world. There was and always will be, art being created by artists locally, but then, it was well-known that Paris was the place where artists had migrated to improve their skills and be a part of something special.

Perhaps, I'm more the exception than the rule. I never really had any plans on being a painter myself. Such desires often push a person to study art history. Yet, there are still too many of us non-painters that are searching for the few jobs that are available in our expertise. Now that I'm in my senior year I'm trying to figure out how I can stay in Paris, as well as get a masters and also a plan for making a living. Some days, making this all happen seems about as likely as my fulfilling my desire to just move into the D'Orsay.

My parents have let me know that I'm on my own after they had funded the one year in Paris that expanded to four. The seventh arrondissement is rich in galleries. After all, we are home to *Carre Rive Gauche, Antiquaires & Galeries D'Art*—an association that gives us some extra prestige. Today I gave my resume to three galleries, *Francois Belliad, Pia* and *Jantzen*. They seemed to think that since my French was good enough, and because English was my native language, I might be a benefit for their clientele. Thank God for the University program of arranged housing with Parisian families. "*Ma famille*," truly adopted me. I imagine I would not have made it four years without the kindness and affordability of living with them. They have already let me know that I can stay, provided that, I can work out a way of remaining in Paris. I did enjoy progressively helping with their two young kids. Ah, life's trade-offs. As much as this arrangement was essential for my being in Paris and obtaining a degree, living with a family has put some restrictions on any relationship interests. I didn't terribly mind. The socialization within the classroom of the various campuses was enough for me. Not to mention that my heart was already enchanted by the titans of Impressionism, Post-Impressionism, and the Fauves. I should be able to make ends meet for one more year, while I get a masters. Beyond that, the figures still don't add up. My family's apartment is just down the block from *Maison Serge Gainsbourg*, on Rue de Verneuil. I've been listening to his music, and trying to channel some of his artistic energy. It seems that this cooky Jewish boy, turned everything he touched to gold. Of course, I don't have his talent, but for four years I've been absorbing the works of his genius. I have this delusion, that perhaps, if I keep channeling Gainsbourg's addictive craziness and mix it with all that I've learned from the master creators, possibly, some sort of inspiration will come out of me. Maybe I will find something or some way, that I can continue to be emersed in my passion—which, would include moving into the D'Orsay. Ha, ha, dream on girl. I have so intensely imagined this fantasy that I could write a book that mimics this idea. Hey, wait, why not? AUP has toned my writing skills. Wow, I like it. I can find a way to incorporate in, the other icons of the seventh, such as the Eiffel tower! Oh, and Invalides and the Rodin Museum. This could be fun. Thanks for listening, I've got to go. I'm off to my room and my headphones, with my Ipod set to Gainsbourg. Don't forget, you are the witness of the conceiving of 'The Girl who lived in the D'Orsay.'

5/2022

Jeanne
ARTBZ.BZ

SKETCHBOOK – PARIS

SKETCHBOOK – PARIS

135

SKETCHBOOK – PARIS

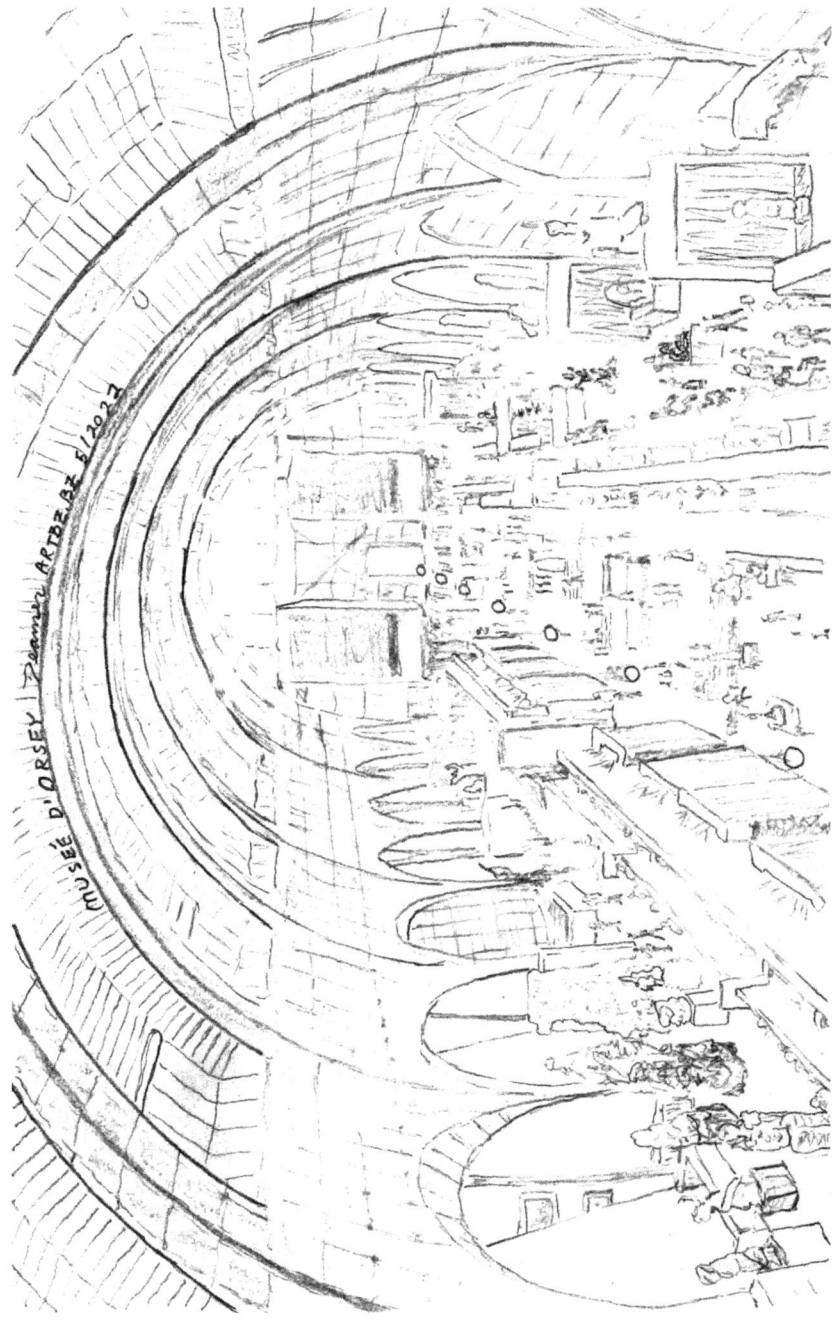

8th Arrondissement

My first trip to Paris happened when I was still a college student. My father was on a diplomatic mission for our country, Malta. He had accommodation at the luxury hotel of *Prince des Galles,* which is located on the famed *Avenue George V.* I showed up with two of my college friends and crashed in the room's suite. I got the couch, while my friends found comfort on the lush, carpeted floor. With today's awareness of security, I doubt that we would ever have been let in the hotel. Even back then, we had to wait in the lobby until my father came down and identified me as his daughter.

Funny how fate can be. I have lived in Paris now for twenty-years, as the wife of the Malta ambassador. Despite my father's diplomatic history, adjusting to this life was quite an accomplishment. You must understand that I was the kind of little girl who ran around the island with no shoes and little care. It was rather rare to catch me in anything other than shorts and a sleeveless pullover. Ah, the life of a careless little one on a southern Mediterranean island. That all seems like a different life now. A couple of the other embassy wives took me under their wing and introduced me to all the shops of the *Avenue des Champs-Élysées, George V* and in particular, *Avenue Montagne.* Dior, LV, Channel, Ralph Lauren, Brunello Cucinelli, Fendi, Jimmy Choo, Givenchy, Prada—it's an endless stroll through seemingly endless famous designer names. All of these brands, who are known all over the world, meant nothing to the little girl, who had run around Malta barefooted.

Francoise, as the French call my husband, is twenty years older than I. More and more lately, I've been taking over his duties, which include lunching with visiting dignitaries. The other evening, I even took out a group of men to the topless review at the famed '*Club Crazy Horse.*' In some ways, being with the men, is not so different than being out with the women of the diplomats. There are still plenty of misconceptions about my country that I have to walk around and help others get through, such as, 'Malta, are you a part of Italy or Spain? Do you still have a king? Are you near Mallorca or Corsica?' I do get a kick out of their changes of expression when I inform them that Malta is not only an independent country, it is also further south than the city of Tunis, Tunisia in Africa. For those who are close to our life in Paris, it is rather assumed that one day I will be formally named to replace my husband—perhaps even while he is still alive. But you must understand what a big deal this would be for my country. We are still a patriarchal society, dominated by the church's influence. I've been told by several Maltese people, that there is no way that I will actually get the post. Apparently, some still remember that barefoot fancy-free girl who never showed up to church. There is also the unspoken, yet well-known reality of Malta politics. Positions of authority in Malta rarely change hands without some important person profiting. Our history of corruption is as old as our existence. I've asked my husband how he got the appointment and all he would ever tell me was that I was better off not knowing. For years I just entertained those who rode above or below the clouds, as if they were my best friend. As my husband's health has deteriorated, I have received less and less instructions from him. I'm aware that some of our staff are choosing sides, as well as lobbying the different nuances of the political elite and the authorities of the church. Often, I think of my father these days. I wonder what kind of compromises he had to make, and whom he was able to say yes or no to. One thing I know for sure is that not in his wildest dreams, could he ever have imagined that his daughter, a woman, would someday represent Malta as its ambassador. There will always be days where I long for the open lands of my country, its stark colonial architecture and the particular color of its surrounding sea. But, the time has come, for women to be more of a part of its future, on the island and perhaps even here in Paris.

SKETCHBOOK – PARIS

SKETCHBOOK – PARIS

9th Arrondissement

It is rather random how I ended up in the 9th. I've bounced around Paris like a volleyball looking for some earth to land upon. The first decade of my work career was crazy. I mean how do you plan for a great recession, an epidemic, or a dictator invading Ukraine? For me, it has meant a variety of jobs, which at least has given me a variety of experiences. When I was hired at *Hôtel Drouot*, I also found a flat in the ninth. With all of the recent world chaos, I've hunkered down and truly made this arrondissement the center of my world. After all, the ninth is really the heart of retail in Paris. You can start with my employer, the internationally famed auction house. It originated as one of the first world art galleries. It is crazy to think how this was the same seller, who helped many of the Impressionists survive their early scorn. Back in the Eighteen hundreds, The Drouot had a fairly low-key but prominent corner location. The current building feels more like a fortress, which we believe gives it a grand sense of security—after all, those same impressionists' paintings no longer sell for the price of a good lunch. We deal with works that go for millions, which support our massive staff and influence. A forgotten fact was how our history actually paved the way for the Gare D'Orsay to become the very popular *Musée de D'Orsay*. While we were building our modern building, we held our shows in the old railroad station, which was later renovated into one of the world's great museums.

Of course, when it comes to retail, most Parisians think of Boulevard Haussmann and its French retail Titans. In particular, *Printemps* and *Galleries Lafayette*. Their massive presence and inventory have inspired the global world of retail. I worked for both in my ping pong path to working for the high class Hôtel Drouot. I hope to stay and grow within this impressive organization. There is something more thrilling in being a part of a million-dollar sale, verses, my days of a euro here and there. The Ninth is not just special because of all of its retail. All of this activity supports a plethora of restaurants and cafes. What really endeared me to this arrondissement, is all of its somewhat hidden passageways. They give you a sense of discovery. As a worker, I love making the big sale; as a customer, I love to search for bargains within the passageways. Books, stamps, every type of food and a most interesting selection of art are on display in these ancient pathways that are now mostly covered with glass rooves. They kind of feel like a village within a city. Every time that I venture into the *Passage Jouffroy*, I find something new, something that is particularly endearing. After all, aren't such pursuits some of the best of living?

SKETCHBOOK – PARIS

SKETCHBOOK – PARIS

10th arrondissement

Technology allowed us to move two hours to the east of Paris. We still consider it our city, while living the quieter, simpler country life. Honestly, we had begun to lose our love of this magical city. All of the years that we had battled the challenges of Paris, so that we could make a living, had taken a toll. The crisis of the Covid epidemic had actually turned into a blessing for us. When both of our jobs went remote, we soon realized that we no longer wanted to go back to the daily grind of working in an office. George was able to keep his position and stay remote. I transitioned into one that also allowed me to do most of my work via the Internet. Our kids are grown and living abroad. So, we were able to rent out our Paris apartment and buy a place in the country. In an ironic twist, we have begun to think of the 10th as our new little piece of Paris. In less than two hours, a train zips us into *Gare de L'est*, and *voila*, we are back in Paris. From living on the left bank for so many years, we had found a bit of renewal by exploring the right bank. We still come into town frequently enough that we have become rather familiar with the *Gare de L'est* and its neighborhood. There is that wonderful painting by the American artist, Albert Herter, which spans almost the entire entry. The scene, of the crowding around a train is a memorial to the first World War. It has meant more to us since Europe is again experiencing an invasion. How naive of us to think that we Europeans are beyond the tragedy of conquest. Sometimes I pull out my phone and take a fresh image of this great artwork. Then, on our train ride back to our new home, we try to imagine the scene, the lives, which were so upset by the chaos of war. Our discussion often returns to the stories we hear coming out of Ukraine—how war has changed, how it is still the same…

We have adopted the *Hôtel Les Deux Gares* as a kind of second home. In case you are not familiar with this transit-oriented piece of Paris, The Deux Gares is a reference to the fact that the *Gare de Nord* is just a hop skip and a jump from the *Gare de L'est*, with the hotel, located between the two. We pop out of the train, take a right walk out of the station and then take that wonderful dual stone staircase that transitions us away from the trials of travel and into our new adopted neighborhood. There is something about the Hotel's elevation above the tracks that we find endearing. We are always greeted by name and made to feel like a part of the hotel's family. We know all of the staff's names as well. We have also learned a lot about the crew across the street, at our new favorite restaurant, *Café Les Deux Gares*.

This weekend trip, is all about fun, without us having to leave the tenth. We arrived mid-day and headed for the covered confines to what we refer to as the 'passages.' Passage Brady and its neighbor *Passage de l' Industrie*. First stop, *Sommier* for our costumes and then on to *Schanabelle de Paris*, where I went for a blond wig with green highlights, while fitting my husband with a rather dashing purple one. We were invited to a costume party in the wonderful courtyard of the *Conservatoire Hector Berlioz* on Rue Pierre Bullet. But first, lunch around the corner at *Old Shalimar*, our favorite Indian restaurant. We have a grand time reminiscing of all our visits to the Conservatoire of music, when our daughter attended and graduated. We laugh away as we down all the wonderfully spicy food. How special to rediscover a love of life, our city and each other. All due to a horrific epidemic. What's the old expression? Ah, when given a bowl of lemons, make lemonade.

SKETCHBOOK – PARIS

SKETCHBOOK – PARIS

SKETCHBOOK – PARIS

11th arrondissement

I had the most interesting day, which as always, started on the narrow *Rue Sedaine* in the heart of the Eleventh Arrondissement. My morning began at *Café L'Industrie*, nursing my morning croissant and coffee. I had heard that this part of the city was once considered a real center for the political left, both the communists and socialists. I got a taste of this over-hearing 'oldster' neighbors as they complained about the demise of the movement. They spoke of the big rallies and protests that used to swarm around *Place Bastille* and its memorial to the Revolution of 1830. The more they spit upon today's youth, the crankier they became. What was fascinating to me, at first, became so repetitive and disconnected that eventually I had to suppress some giggles. I slipped a few Euros onto the table and thanked those who were working. It was a perfect segue to go across the street and visit the cats at the *Cafe du Chat*. I know all the kitties by name now, not only because I visit them on a regular basis, I help out with their feeding once in a while.

It is not that I planned to find a home in the Eleventh arrondissement. You might say that it found me. A lover asked me to move in and, well, I said yes. It didn't take me long to settle in and make the apartment on Rue Sedaine feel like home. It wasn't hard, my boyfriend traveled a lot, which gave me time to tweak things here and there. The fact that he didn't come home after one of those trips didn't stop me from adopting the neighborhood that adopted me. For the longest time I kept expecting him to return, but that never happened. What did happen is I kept getting offered odd jobs here and there. Within a year I had worked at quite a variety of shops, restaurants and coffee houses. Word just got around that I was happy to fill-in for anyone who needed some time off. It didn't take long before it seemed everyone knew me and could rely on me to do just about anything that was asked—always with a smile. I really didn't need to leave Rue Sedaine to work or get what I need. The boyfriend had paid the apartment for a year, which really helped me get on my feet by the time it came for me to pay my own way.

Back on Rue Sedaine, it had begun to drizzle but this did not affect my sunny mood, I actually like walking in the rain. I checked the sky; its grey was getting darker. I waved to those inside *Atelier Sedaine*, I loved the painting class I had taken there. Perhaps enough Euros would accumulate so that I could further my skills with a brush. I peeked into *Les Mauvais Joueurs*, a bar surrounded by board games, I love working among this *société de jeux*. Another waive to those inside The *City Pet Shop*, another fun place to fill in. I smiled as I walked past the *Artist Noodle*. I haven't worked there yet, but I sure do enjoy their artistically plated noodles. I hurried across the main thorough fare of Boulevard Voltaire, just out running that little man on the pole, as he turned from green to red. The other day, I finally picked up a book by Voltaire since we not only have this boulevard, but also a *musée* for him. I loved his character Candide. That man seemed to get pushed around as much by fate as this girl. I took a left on Rue Parmentier, since this is where Rue Sedaine ends. It was then that the clouds opened and the rain came. I love to walk in the rain, but this came down so hard that I ducked into a nearby café. I had not been inside before, I wasn't even sure that I had noticed this place. I asked and was told it was called *11eme Avenue*. Typical to this neighborhood it was a mixed crowd, many different faces. Yet, also typical of a Paris café, they seemed to all know each other. I just got a coffee, which nicely out lasted the heavy rain. I returned to the light version, enjoying how it seemed to quieten everything. This always mellows my anxiety, which tends to always brew endlessly like a fire in a dry grassy field.

I never knew my parents. My Grandparents raised me. They are both gone now. Their final resting place is far from Paris. I developed a new habit since I once again found myself living alone. The *Cimetière du Père Lachaise*, Paris's most visited cemetery, is nearby. Technically it is in the bordering twentieth arrondissement, but I like to think of it as part of the Eleventh, a part of my little world. I stop at the *Le Pavillon des Fleurs* and buy a bunch of flowers. I enjoy them like someone gave them to me the whole walk up the hill on Avenue Gambetta. I do visit the more popular graves. Something has been lost in the glassing off of Monsieur Victor Hugo's grave. So many women left their lipstick kisses that they added a layer of separation. You still see kisses left on the plexiglass. They finally fenced off the resting spot for American rocker, Jim Morrison. Though, people still seem to manage and climb over and leave some memento behind. Last time I came by, there was a threesome visiting the 'Sparrow,' Edith Piaf, and playing some of her songs in respect. I enjoyed that. What I like to do most is make a new friend. I find a random grave, clean it up and top it with the flowers. I introduce myself, tell them a version of my life on Rue Sedaine and promise to return. I tell them about my elders, suggesting that they might look out for them. I promise to return, though, I'm usually too twisted around to be able to find to any particular spot, any grave site, any marker of a life now gone…

SKETCHBOOK – PARIS

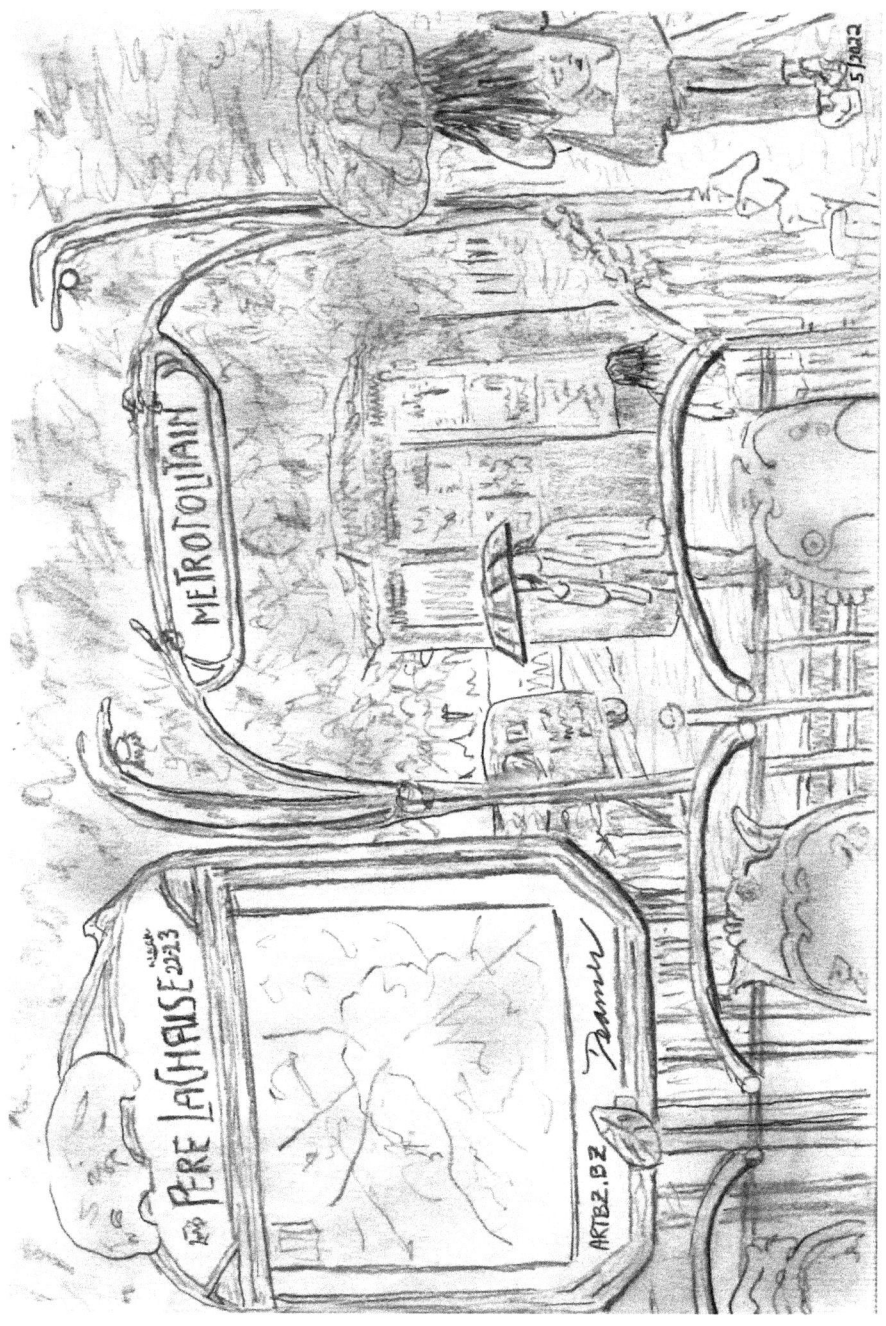

SKETCHBOOK – PARIS

BASTILLE 5/2022

12th arrondissement

We all know that sound. Maybe not when you first hear it rolling toward you, but soon we figure it out. It is crazy to think that this particular sound of a society on the move didn't even exist until a while ago. Oh sure, the wheel has been around since it was considered one of man's first revolutionary inventions. But now, at least when we travel, we hear the sound of a human pulling a suitcase on wheels. You probably laugh at this whole thought, but you will understand when I explain that I live in an apartment right above one of the world's busiest train stations, the *Gare Lyon*. If you are going south in France by train, chances are, you'll be walking through my line of sight, perhaps participating in the orchestra of rolling wheels. There are more than travelers that occupy *Place Henri Frenay*. There are quite a few of us that live in the adjacent buildings and we are not opposed to joining all the travelers in visiting the businesses that align this grand plaza. It is quite a luxury to have all these offerings without having to take on any traffic in the nearby streets. I don't mind sharing our local bistro with travelers. *L'Espanade* is not a fancy restaurant, but I find it convenient that they offer such a variety of choices. They serve up French fare with some ethnic twists. Basically, it's comfort food, for a traveler or for a weary resident. The plaza is not just a conduit for the station. Many children enjoy playing in this big, open space, as well as those who covet an outdoor sanctuary. I find it all entertaining, whether from my window or when I'm on the patio of the café.

It's not that I chose to live in the twelfth for any romantic reason; it was all very practical. When I took the job that I couldn't turn down, it meant leaving Provence behind and finally moving to our capital. There was no wife to worry about, I was divorced. But my mother always feared the day that I would leave. Part of my reassurance was that by living next to the station I was just a few hours away from her. Well, at least if I caught one of the express trains. The other carrot I dangled for her was that when she visited, I would to take her to the opera or any other event that might interest her at nearby Bercy. As much as she likes a Paris dinner and the walk to the opera house facing the bastille, she seems to have even more fun when we walk in the opposite direction to *Cinematheque*. This cinema, within the dramatic Frank Gehry designed building, shows the old movies that she so cherished. It was rather ironic how I had worked so hard to convince her that I would come visit almost every weekend. It didn't take long for that idea to reverse itself, when she preferred to come visit me.

It all worked out well until along came the pandemic. I didn't mind the move to working at home, I'm still doing it most of the time. All this time alone, looking down on the travelers did bring on more thoughts about life. Like pondering the sounds of people pulling and pushing their stuff on wheels. Covid made Ma afraid to travel, I was afraid to visit and bring the virus with me. In the end, she got the virus anyway, passing alone in her room. Her funeral and the cleaning out of our house was a lonely business as well. I still expect the phone to ring and hear all those same questions she would ask me over and over. It was her way as a mother to feel reassured that her son was okay.

I started a new habit to assist my mental health. Each day I extend my lunch break away from the home computer and enjoy the *Coulée verte René-Dumont*. This conversion of an old above ground rail line into a walking park, is a magnificent local resource of green, with unique elevated views. With all the crowds drawn to our Gare and event halls, walking this unique park is a very meditative experience. At first, we were all still wearing our masks, which seemed such an oxymoron for this nature walk. Gradually, we all started to remove the masks and look upon each other's personalities again. My mother is still in my mind. In particular, I hear her commenting on any women walking alone or sitting with their lunch. A couple of times, I've caught myself responding to my thoughts of ma out loud. I know that I need to make more of an effort in getting a woman back in my life. I started by making eye contact and saying a simple bonjour as I passed.

Something kind of magical happened yesterday. As much as I would feel my mother trying to push me to sit near certain female 'lunchers,' I could never find the nerve to get very close. Yesterday, this friendly gal, also from Provence, sat down right next to me and started engaging me like we had known each other since we were kids. She laughed, stating she lived on the narrow street of Rue Sedaine in the eleventh arrondissement. She had also decided that it was time for her to start reaching out more. We ended up sharing some of the foods we brought, and well, we have a date for some more lunch sharing tomorrow…

SKETCHBOOK – PARIS

SKETCHBOOK – PARIS

SKETCHBOOK – PARIS

197

14th arrondissement - Montparnasse

Much has been made of the competition of the cafés of *Vavin*. We Parisians have had over a century to argue about who is the best. Is it *La Coupole, Le Select, La Rotonde* or *Le Dôme*? With these four Titans of the neighborhood of *Vavin* within the 14th arrondissement of Montparnasse all being a stone's throw from each other, it has been a long, never-ending discussion. Technically, *La Rotonde* and *Le Select* are on the other side of the arrondissement line putting them in the 6th. But we locals consider all the *Vavin*, which straddles both, as being the heart of Montparnasse. So much of the life of Montparnasse goes on beyond the *Vavin*, but it is within these four cafés that those things most memorable, seem to happen—such as falling in or out of love. This competition so disturbed me that I decided to just split things up each decade. You see, I've been around a while. In the sixties, for my usual hangout, I would frequent *La Coupole*. In the seventies I moved down the street to *Le Dôme*. In the eighties I went across the street to *La Rotonde* and for the nineties I settled into *Le Select*. I never expected to live beyond the millennium change, so once it was upon us, I decided to go wherever my whim took me. Honestly, I don't go out much anymore, even though I live just a block from these iconic cafés.

You might say I was born to be a citizen of Montparnasse, since so much of my life has resembled the history of this Parisian neighborhood. When I was young and pretty, I was a sought-after model. For reasons I never really understood or cared about, I was just as comfortable naked as I was dressed up. Painters and photographers seemed to appreciate this, which also seemed to help keep me working as well as bouncing from lover to lover. My lifestyle so resembled the famed, "Queen of Montparnasse," the turn of the century model, known as "Kiki," that people started calling me by her nickname as well. I even identified with the building of the Montparnasse Tower in the late nineteen-sixties. You see, I was quite tall and my lifestyle always quite controversial, so we seemed to be cut from the same mold. I found myself as the rare local who would defend its creation. Partially due to our resemblance, and because I always did like to take the other side of any argument. As my often photographed and painted body began to loosen with the years, I switched over to the other side of the camera and canvas.

Over the years I found myself drawn to artists of all kinds. There was a grand creative group that lingered around Montparnasse and the well-known resident film making couple, Agnus Varda and Jacque Demy. All these acquaintances helped me continue to make a life in Montparnasse within the arts. I began experimenting on my own, as well as with my artistic friends that enjoyed encouraging me. I had some success selling works of art and photography. But even more important to me is how this pursuit became my best friend as I got older. As this neighborhood's popularity grew, it became more expensive. It was my devotion to the arts that helped me stay. The arrondissement opened a whole apartment building to us older artists with studios to work in and even a gallery to sell our work. Once again, fate surrounded me with those with a passion for the arts. Ah Montparnasse, home to so many great artists. Soutine, Modigliani, Brancusi and Rodin, to name a few—the great existentialist writers, Simone de Beauvoir and Jean Paul Satre lie in rest next to each other in *Cimetière du Montparnasse*. Now, I think these old bones need to go out for lunch. Hmm, which will it be? *La Coupole, Le Dôme, La Rotonde* or *Le Select*?

SKETCHBOOK – PARIS

SKETCHBOOK – PARIS

213

SKETCHBOOK – PARIS

SKETCHBOOK – PARIS

18th arrondissement – Montmartre

I'm convinced that in my previous life, I was one of the Fauves, the Paris painters at the turn of the last century. From the first day I entered Montmartre, I felt like I had been there before. It was more than familiar; I knew it had been important in my past. I was in my twenties when I arrived to Paris, already living and working in five other European countries. I had always sketched, as a child and as a traveler. Once settled into an apartment on the hill, I dove into the colors that I was certain to have used when 'I was a Fauve.' You might be surprised at all the color that is actually a part of our skin and hair. Painters had always included a rich palate of color in their subjects, the Fauves just flipped things around, making color more important than all the neutrals we associate with our being. Even with Montmartre becoming more associated with the next generation of painters led by Picasso, for me, it is the Fauves that will always be a symbol of this neighborhood. Matisse was a full-on participant in the Fauves style and Picasso clearly appreciated what had been going on just before his arrival.

I'm hesitant to continue telling my story, thinking you will think I'm just a typical oldster who complains about how things are today. Montmartre is different, a living tourist designation. I can't complain, it's the tourists that allowed me to live and work here. For fifty years I've made the short walk with my easel and paints, setting up shop in *Place du Tertre*. I could not begin to tell you how many faces I've painted over all these years. I don't know if I should feel proud or ashamed. I know one thing for sure, my original works are hanging in a lot more households than the canvases of Senior Picasso. Is there any square, anywhere in the world, the produces more art than within these few blocks? I don't think so. Even with the sacred white stones of *Sacre Coeur* overseeing us, you could say that art is the true religion of this hill.

For the past twenty or so years, the one thing we could count on was that each year there would be more visitors and our rents would also increase. It is amazing that I'm still here, though staying in the same place for fifty years can slow the rent increases to some degree. I can't believe it's been fifty years. I always thought I would return to traveling, but somehow it never was convenient. We have such a community among us artists. When I came to Montmartre, I found my family. I've had some relations over the years, but they never lasted. Perhaps, because art would always be my true love. And, well, I've always had an issue with drinking. There is a whole culture of finishing the day with drinks and conversation. We get to sharing and laughing about our daily painting conquests and it is just so easy to keep lifting a glass in cheer. It wasn't until, oh, maybe twenty years ago that I started drinking at home as well. There are just days when I can't get up and make the walk. I am tired, pretty much all the time. At least, I gave fifty years to the tradition of the Fauves, bringing out the color in all the faces that sat before me. About a year ago, I gave up on paint, its cost, its poisonous chemicals. It is kind of ironic don't you think? In coming to Montmartre, I found a life within the colors of paint, only to realize that its make-up would slowly kill the life in me. Friends still look in on me and I can

SKETCHBOOK – PARIS

always put on Django Reinhart. His music remains one of my longest relationships. I imagine his music will bounce around this hilltop even longer than either you or me. On good days I make it to the *Place de Tertre* with my charcoals. My hands are a little shaky, but I can still achieve a great impression with just a few strokes. Well, at least most of the time. On occasion, I still see that look in a client's eyes when they watch me draw and learn that I have lived in Montmartre for virtually my whole life. For me, it feels like envy—some even verbalize it. This, along with all the memories keeps me going. Even on the bad days, I know I wouldn't have changed anything…

SKETCHBOOK – PARIS

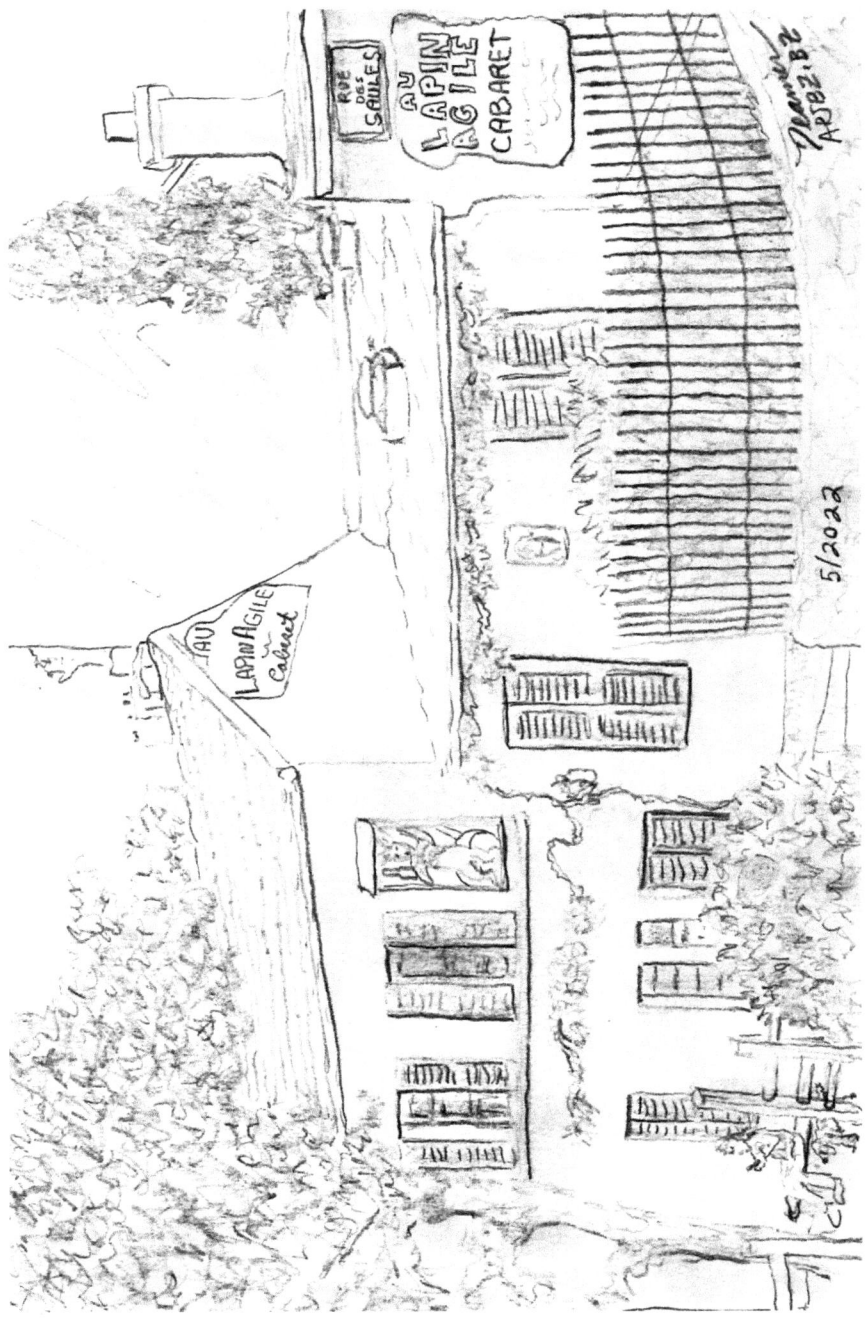

SKETCHBOOK – PARIS

SKETCHBOOK – PARIS

SKETCHBOOK – PARIS

DEAMER DUNN artbz.bz

STORIES, IMAGES & BLANK PAGES FOR YOU BY ARRONDISSEMENT

4.	Juveniles	89.	Ma Bourgogne
6.	**1st**	91.	Place du Vosges
7.	Tuileries Eiffel	**92.**	**5th**
9.	Musee du Louvre	95.	Shakespeare & Co
11.	Le Tub Outside	97.	Creperie Mouffetard
13.	Nomad	99.	Papilla & the Pantheon
15.	L'Entracte	101.	Rue Mouffetard
17.	Le Tubb Inside	103.	Tram & La Dame
19.	Moi Pho	105.	Lib Galarie de la Sorbonne
21.	Maceo	**106.**	**6th**
23.	Jardin du Palais	107.	Les Deux Magots Inside
25.	Au Pied de Cochon	109.	Café de Flore
27.	Royal Vendome	111.	Coffee Cart
29.	Presto Fresco Pizza	113.	Les Deux Magots Outside
31.	St Honore Marche	115.	Vulpian Sculpture&Neighborhood
33.	Florist	117.	Le Saint Andre
34.	**2nd**	119.	Parc Luxembourg
35.	Vaudeville	121.	Closerie des Lilas
37.	Boufes Parisan	123.	San Francisco Books
39.	Café du Cadran	125.	Librarie Poesie
41.	Brasserie Dubillot	127.	Assouline Librarie
43.	Ma Cave Fleury	**128.**	**7th**
45.	La Cordonnerie	129.	Trocadero Eiffel
47.	Culottee Café	131.	American University of Paris
48.	**3rd**	133.	Galerie Jantzen & PLA
49.	MER-Corossole	135.	Tabac L'Universite
51.	Place de la Republic	137.	L'Esperance
53.	Big Love Vegetarian	139.	Rodin's Le Pensieur
55.	Aux Crus Bourgogne	141.	Musee´ D'Orsay
57.	MER-Chez Alain	**142.**	**8th**
59.	MER-Au Coin Bio	143.	Prince de Galles
61.	MER-Chez Taeko	145.	Ralph Lauren
63.	Le Sancerre	147.	Chanel22
65.	Unicorners Cafe	149.	Versace
67.	Carrette Place du Vosges	151.	Champs Elysées
68.	**4th**	**152.**	**9th**
71.	Notre Dame Artists	153.	Librairie du Passage
73.	L' Ebouillante	155.	Les Vergers Cadet
75.	Pont de le Tounelle	157.	Grevin Musée
77.	Au Vieux Paris d'Arcole	159.	Monblue Formage Restaurant
79.	Creperie Bobo	161.	Passage Jouffroy
81.	Gribouille	**162.**	**10th**
83.	Eataly Paris	163.	Gare de L'Est
85.	Le Floreen Lile	165.	Old Shalmer
87.	Place Beaubourg	167.	Taka Vermo Cheese

SKETCHBOOK – PARIS

169. Altermundi & Astre
171. Mural Rue Cite Riverin
172. 11th
173. Eleventh Avenue
175. Le Café du Chat
177. Café Lindustrie
179. Metro Pere La Chaise
181. Pere La Chaise Edith Piaf
183. Altier Sedaine
185. Bastille
186. 12th
187. Gare Lyon
189. Parisil
191. Boulangerie Viennois
193. Parc Bercy
195. Coulée Verte Rene Dumont
197. Le Singe a Paris
199. Bistro tdu Coin
200. 14th
201. Le Dôme
203. Le Select
205. La Coupole
207. Café de La Rotonde
209. Top of Tower
211. Eiffel from Tower
213. Edgar Quinet Rue de la Gaite´
215. Maison Fadoro
217. Produce Marchier
219. Cafe' Odessa
220. 18th
221. La Virgule & Sacre Cœur
223. Lapin Agile
225. Cimentiere de Saint Vincent
227. Place du Tertre Eiffel Art
229. Place du Tertre Portrait
231. Pigalle
233. Rue Cortot
235. La Bonne Franquette

Deamer Sketchbooks:

In case you haven't heard, coloring books for all ages are becoming quite a passion. Perhaps, for many, a little coloring can still feed a passion for getting into a book, as well as allowing the satisfaction of finishing something. A few sketches are accompanied with a fictional story inspired by the scene. Deamer Sketchbooks are meant to inspire you. Each sketch is partnered with a blank page—you can add notes, comments, poems, words of a song, or your own artistic doodles—innovation inspired by creative human activity. The idea is that this is a book that you can make your own. It is a travel companion, whether you take it along, or it takes you…

Available Deamer Sketchbooks:

SAN DIEGO, SAN DIEGO: LITTLE ITALY MERCATO, CENTRAL COAST CALIFORNIA, CHERRYBEAN COFFEE, SALINAS CA, TIJUANA MEXICO (DUAL LANGUAGE BOOK), UMBRIA, ITALY, SAN FRANCISCO, *MUSEUM OF MODERN ART SAN FRANCISCO*, **SKETCH/COOKBOOK PS GRILL**, NEW YORK CITY, *MUSEUM OF MODERN ART NYC*, HAVANA CUBA, HONG KONG, MAIN STREET SALINAS, MARKET DAY CARMEL, SEATTLE, LAS VEGAS, LUGANO SWITZERLAND, PARIS, & *MUSEE D'ORSAY PARIS*

Coming Soon:
MIAMI, SALT LAKE CITY, SANTA FE, AUSTIN TX, NEW ORLEANS

Being Researched:
BERLIN, VIENNA, PRAGUE, BUDHAPEST, RIO DE JANERIO, BUENOS AIRES, BOGOTA COLOMBIA, SINGAPORE, BANGKOK, TOKYO, INSTANBUL, SOUTH AFRICA, SYDNEY, NEW ZEALAND

You can also follow and/or view all the Deamer Sketchbook sketches in images & music videos:

https://www.youtube.com/channel/deamerdunn
and/or
https://www.instagram.com/deamerauthor/

Novels by Deamer:
Pickup a Deamer novel online or from your local bookstore:
https://www.amazon.com/author/deamerdunn

STRENGTH AND GRACE
Winner, one of best fiction novels of 2015
Southern California Book Festival & Great Midwest Book Festival
Also available in Spanish:
FUERZA y GRACIA (Español)

MEETANDTELL.COM/ADVENTURE
Winner, one of best romance novels of 2016
Los Angeles Book Festival

Omar T Series (Culinary Adventures)
TRAVEL FICTION

Omar and his family travel to a different location for each of these culinary adventures. The travel fiction aspect is enhanced with descriptions of actual sites, restaurants, bookstores, galleries and shops—including sketches, favorite lists and recipes. Diversity in race, religion, culture, language and sexual orientation not only exists within Omar's family, it is celebrated in these tales. Each Omar T book is independent, you do not need to read them in the order of their publication, though, as the collection grows, there are more references between the novels.

Available now: Monterey California, San Diego/Tijuana, Umbria Italy, San Francisco, New York City, Havana Cuba, Hong Kong, Seattle & Las Vegas
In the Works: Miami, Austin Texas, New Orleans and Lugano Switzerland
Being researched: Santa Fe NM, Berlin, Buenos Aries, Rio, Singapore, Bangkok, Istanbul, Africa *and then????*

About the Author/Artist

Chef Deamer was born and raised in Salt Lake City, Utah. He lived in Switzerland and the Washington D.C. area before settling in Monterey County California in the early 1980's. "I had the incredible luxury of having a world class artist for a mother. Gradually some of her skills rubbed off on me." Deamer maintains a home in the birth city of John Steinbeck, Salinas California, the former location of his dinner only restaurant, Pajaro Street Grill. Deamer now spends much of his time in Tijuana Mexico and traveling the world with his recurring character, Omar T Black. "I have a list of some thirty more locations where I hope to write Omar adventures– come join the journey!"

http://artbz.bz

"Everyday is a great day to read a book or color one!!!"

Keep in touch with Deamer, as Omar travels the world, deamer@artbz.bz Please pass on your impressions; write a review on Amazon and/or other sites such as Goodreads – your thoughts can really make a difference! Just about any bookstore, anywhere in the world, can get you a Deamer book through Ingram at the same price as Amazon ☺ https://www.amazon.com/author/deamerdunn You can also support your local bookstore via: https://bookshop.org/shop/deamerdunn

Romantic, Novelist, Obsessive Traveler, Sketchaholic

www.ingramcontent.com/pod-product-compliance
Lightning Source LLC
LaVergne TN
LVHW010315070526
838199LV00065B/5575